P9-CBT-104

Style Secrets

HAIR
CARE

TIPS & TRICKS

KAREN LATCHANA KENNEY

ILLUSTRATED BY ELENA HESCHKE

Lerner Publications ◆ Minneapolis

Text and illustrations copyright © 2016 by Lerner Publishing Group, Inc.

All rights reserved. International copyright secured. No part of this book may be reproduced, stored in a retrieval system, or transmitted in any form or by any means—electronic, mechanical, recording, or otherwise—without the prior written permission of Lerner Publishing Group, Inc., except for the inclusion of brief quotations in an acknowledged review.

Lerner Publications Company
A division of Lerner Publishing Group, Inc.
241 First Avenue North
Minneapolis, MN 55401 USA

For reading levels and more information, look up this title at www.lernerbooks.com.

Main body text set in Grotesque MT Std. Light 10/14.
Typeface provided by Monotype.

Library of Congress Cataloging-in-Publication Data

Kenney, Karen Latchana
    Hair care tips & tricks / by Karen Latchana Kenney ; illustrated by Elena Heschke.
        pages   cm. — (Style Secrets)
    Includes index.
        ISBN 978-1-4677-5218-3 (lib. bdg. : alk. paper)
        ISBN 978-1-4677-8653-9 (EB pdf)
        1. Hairstyles—Juvenile literature. 2. Hair—Care and hygiene—Juvenile literature. 3. Grooming for girls—Juvenile literature. I. Title. II. Title: Hair care tips and tricks.
    TT972.H846 2016
    646.7'24—dc23   2014012480

Manufactured in the United States of America
1 – VP – 7/15/15

CONTENTS

Introduction

HAIR TALK

Do you wish you had perfect hair? Doesn't everybody? The thing is, there is no such thing as perfect hair. We all have good and bad hair days. Sometimes hair has a mind of its own, whether it's totally limp or all frizz. But with some products, tools, time, and personal style, your hair can be perfectly *you*.

What does it take to have great hair? Healthy habits, regular cuts, and the right tools are a good start. Different products protect hair, add shine, and keep styles in place. And personalized accessories make any hairstyle extra special.

Ready to see where your style takes you? Use some simple tips and tricks to try something new. You can make your hair healthy, interesting, and fun!

Chapter 1
HEALTHY HAIR

Hair comes in many textures and types. But one thing's true for all hair: it looks best when it's healthy. If you take good care of your hair, it'll look great naturally and will be much easier to style.

So how do you keep your hair healthy? For starters, you need to know your hair type. Look closely at a strand of hair. Is it thick and wiry? Or is it thin and fragile? Pull on it. Does it break—or bounce back to its normal shape? This tells you about your hair's texture. Coarse hair is heavy, thick, and a little wiry. It's often frizzy, has a lot of body, and may break easily. Medium hair is not too thick or thin. It's strong and keeps its shape. Thin hair can be strong or weak, but it has very fine strands. That's why thin hair often looks limp.

Next, feel your hair and check it out under the light. Does it feel silky smooth or brittle and dry? Does it shine or look dull? This helps you categorize your hair in a different way. It could be dry, normal, oily, or combination hair. Your scalp produces oil to keep your hair healthy and moist. Sometimes the scalp makes too much or too little oil, though. Too little oil leaves hair dry, dull, and hard to manage. Too much oil makes hair limp and sticky. Some people have oily roots and dry ends. That's combination hair. And what about the people who seem to have way more good hair days than bad ones? They have "normal" hair with just the right balance of oil.

Once you've figured out your hair texture and type, you can pick products and treatments that will help your hair look its best. It's especially important to find a shampoo and conditioner that's targeted at your hair type. Shampoos cleanse your scalp and hair. Conditioners moisturize your hair. Some add body and bounce. Others add extra moisture and shine.

HONEY COCONUT HAIR MASK

A hair mask is a deep conditioning treatment for your hair. Try using it once a week in place of your regular conditioner. You'll give your hair an extra dose of the nutrients it needs, which will amp up its shine and softness. This mask is made from natural ingredients: honey and coconut oil. Coconut oil is a solid form of oil you can find in the natural foods section of a grocery store or a co-op.

What You Need:

- a towel
- measuring spoons
- 1 tablespoon (14.8 milliliters) honey
- 1 tablespoon coconut oil
- a microwave-safe bowl
- a mixing spoon
- a shower cap

Here's How:

1. Put a towel around your shoulders and get your hair damp.

2. Measure the honey and coconut oil into the bowl. Mix well.

3. Heat the mixture in the microwave for 30 seconds or until warm. Don't heat it too much!

4. Apply the mask to your hair. Rub it into your ends and roots.

5. If you have long or medium-length hair, wrap it into a bun. Put on your shower cap and wait for 30 to 40 minutes.

6. In the shower, rinse the mask out of your hair. Then use your normal shampoo and conditioner. What's the result? Soft, shiny, and smooth hair.

STYLING PRODUCTS

Even when your hair is clean and healthy, it won't take care of itself. You might wake up with wild frizz or bed head flatness. Styling products can help you tame and even transform your hair. Here are a few common ones to check out:

Hair spray. This sticky spray makes sure your style will last. It comes in different degrees of hold—from weightless to extra firm.

Heat protection. The harsh heat of styling tools—like straighteners and curling irons—can damage your hair. These sprays, creams, and lotions go on right before you add some heat. They help keep hair moist.

Thickeners. These gels and lotions add body to fine hair. When applied to damp roots, hair gains volume as it dries.

Sculpting gels. These thick gels hold hair firmly in place. They can make distinct curls or sculpted bangs. They're great for mohawks and faux hawks too.

Serums and glossers. Once hair is dry, you can give it some extra smoothness and shine. Serums and glossers coat the hair to make it lie smoothly and reflect light. They come in both spray and gel forms.

Waxes and pomades. These products softly define and smooth hair. You can use them to slick your hair back or emphasize curls and ends.

Products can add small touches or help make big statements. But too much can start to weigh your hair down. Don't use too many styling products at once—or even too much of one product. Just a little may be all your hair needs. And even if you don't go overboard, use shampoos or rinses that remove product buildup. Getting rid of buildup restores your hair to its best.

DEEP-CLEANING RINSE

Get rid of product gunk with a deep-cleaning rinse. This one is natural and simple to make. Use it instead of your regular shampoo to bring back your hair's bounce and shine! But save it for rare times when your hair looks really dull. It can be harsh on your hair if used too often. And if you color your hair, be careful. This rinse can strip color.

What You Need:

- a small bowl
- a measuring cup
- $\frac{1}{2}$ cup (118 mL) apple cider vinegar
- $\frac{1}{2}$ cup distilled water
- peppermint, rosemary, or other essential oil (optional)
- a mixing spoon
- a spray bottle

Here's How:

1. Pour the vinegar into the bowl. Add the distilled water. If using essential oils, add a few drops to give the mixture a fun scent. Mix well.

2. Pour the mixture into the spray bottle and reattach the lid tightly.

3. Spray the rinse onto the roots of your hair. Make sure your roots are soaked with the rinse.

4. Massage the rinse down to your ends.

5. Wash the rinse out with cold water in your bathroom sink.

STYLING TOOLS

When it comes to styling your hair, the right tool can be your best friend—and the wrong one can make bad hair worse. If you know what to look for, you can pick the basics that are right for you. Your hair will thank you for it!

Brushes. There are two basic types of brushes—synthetic and natural. Synthetic bristles are made of nylon or polyester. They're fine for working out a few tangles. But natural bristles made of wood or boar hair are gentler on hair. They also help spread oil evenly through hair. That's a win for your hair's health *and* its looks. Boar hairbrushes are expensive, but you can find cheaper brushes with a mix of real hair and nylon bristles. For curly hair, try a brush with a magnesium core. When you use this brush with a hair dryer, the core heats up to add extra hold.

Combs. Wide-tooth combs are great for detangling wet hair. The long handle of a rat-tail comb helps create precise parts. Hair picks are good for very curly or textured hair. They don't get stuck in curls.

Curlers. Curling irons come in wide or narrow barrels. Small, tight curls need a smaller barrel, while a large barrel is great for big waves. Finer hair may not need much heat, but high heat helps smooth out coarse hair. Heated rollers or rods make tight or loose curls. If you have some extra time, use unheated rollers. They take a while to set, but they're healthier for your hair than heat-based products.

Hair dryers. These heated tools create big changes in little time. But they're not all alike. Check out the wattage. More watts equal a faster drying time. Ionic hair dryers use ions to dry extra fast.

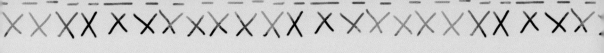

You may have to try a few different types of products and tools before you find the best fit for your hair. If you can, start by borrowing some items from friends or family members. Once you know what works for you, you can do some smart shopping.

Stop the Breakage!

Breakage is a bad word when it comes to hair. It's when hair breaks off in various spots on your head. It often happens to people who have curly and coarse hair. To prevent breakage, follow these tips:

- Don't pull hair too tightly into a ponytail or a bun. And try to switch up the spots on your head where you pull your hair.

- Use hair ties that don't have metal on them. Metal pulls on and breaks hair.

- Don't brush your hair when it's wet. Instead, use a comb to gently work through tangles.

- Avoid using too much heat on your hair. Air-dry your hair as often as possible. And don't use hot tools every day.

- Get regular haircuts. Split ends cause breaks farther up on the strands.

- Condition, condition, condition! Moisturized hair is less likely to break.

Chapter 2

THE RIGHT CUT

Haircuts are *really* important. They remove fragile ends before splits or breakage can occur, and they set a styling base. The right cut suits your hair type and texture. It also suits your face shape. There are five main face shapes—and yours can help you decide what kind of haircut will look best on you.

A <u>square face</u> has a wide forehead and an angular jaw. Soft, layered cuts help to soften the look of this face's sharp lines. Long layers, wavy curls, and side parts work well on someone with a square face.

A <u>round face</u> is as wide as it is tall. Short cuts and short bangs flatter a round face. So do feathered cuts that make hair fall toward the face.

Square

Round

If you have wide cheekbones, a pointy chin, and a narrow forehead, you have an <u>oval face</u>. Almost any haircut looks good with this type of face. So choose one that makes the most of your favorite feature. Bangs emphasize your eyes. Short cuts help cheekbones stand out.

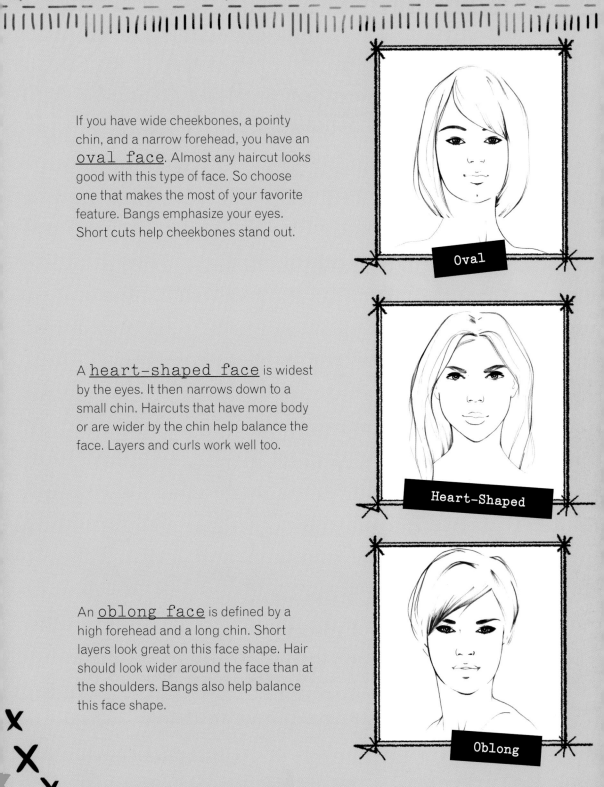

Oval

A <u>heart-shaped face</u> is widest by the eyes. It then narrows down to a small chin. Haircuts that have more body or are wider by the chin help balance the face. Layers and curls work well too.

Heart-Shaped

An <u>oblong face</u> is defined by a high forehead and a long chin. Short layers look great on this face shape. Hair should look wider around the face than at the shoulders. Bangs also help balance this face shape.

Oblong

LENGTH, LENGTH, LENGTH

Long hair always seems to be in style. It flatters most faces, except some oval faces. You can add lots of long, wispy layers. Or you can keep it sleek and chic. There are many ways to vary the long look. Here are a few:

Bangs. Bangs can be bold and thick for lots of drama. They can also be thin and wispy.

Curls. Long hair can be perfect for wavy curls. Thicker hair will need some spray or gel to stay in place all day. If your hair resists your efforts to curl it, don't despair. Just let it settle into bouncy, natural waves.

Layers. A stylist can give you a layered haircut, with shorter lengths of hair closer to the top of your head and a longer base underneath. Layers give hair movement. They also take out some of the weight in coarse and thick hair.

Tousle. For a grungy look, shave one side and leave the rest long. (Or pin some hair back to create the illusion of a partial shave.) If you want your hair to stay in place but still look textured and messy, try a beach spray made of sea salts.

Volume. To add volume on long, thin hair, use big rollers. Spritz some hair spray on the roots. Then back-comb a bit. It makes hair extra big!

Long and Frizzy

If you have frizzy or coarse hair, take extra care of your hair while it grows. Moisturize it well and comb it gently. When it gets to the length you like, you'll need to battle the frizz. Use serums to smooth it. And if your hair is very thick, ask your stylist to thin it out. This will take out the bulk while leaving the length.

NO-CUT BANGS

Love the look of bangs but don't want to commit to the cut? Try some faux bangs for a day. This look is best for long or medium-length hair. If your hair is naturally curly, straighten it first.

What You Need:

- a ponytail holder
- bobby pins
- a curling iron
- a mirror

Here's How:

1. Put your hair in a high ponytail in the middle of your head.

2. Split the ponytail in half across its width. Pull the top half of the ponytail forward.

3. Position the ends of this hair so that they cover your forehead. Pin the hair in place just below the ponytail holder.

4. Wrap the rest of your hair around the ponytail holder to make a bun. Pin that hair in place.

5. Curl the ends of your new "bangs" slightly under or slightly to the side.

6. Gently brush or comb the "bangs" to make them look natural. See what you think!

Clip-Back Bangs

For a different look, create simple sideswept bangs. Make a low side part in your hair. Sweep the top part of your hair over your forehead. Pin that hair behind or just above your ear.

15

SHORT AND MEDIUM CUTS

Your hair doesn't have to be long to make a statement. Short hair can give you a neat, carefree look. A medium cut, ending between the chin and the shoulders, can be casual yet classy.

You don't need to get expensive haircuts to try different lengths. Just experiment at home to create the look of different lengths. Try some updos that give the illusion of a shorter cut. Or add some clip-in extensions to get some more length. There's a lot you can do to play with your look!

CLIP-IN HAIR EXTENSIONS

Do you have short or medium hair but want it to be longer for a day? Make your own extensions to add instant length and thickness! To get started, check out a beauty supply store to get a weft of temporary hair and a package of wig clips.

What You Need:

- a packet of synthetic or human hair, of your preferred length and color, in a weft
- a measuring tape
- scissors
- a mini hot glue gun
- wig clips
- thread the same color as the hair
- a hair clip or hairpins

Here's How:

1. Unroll one end of the weft. It makes a very thin, long layer of hair.

2. Measure the part of your head where you want to add hair.

3. Cut three widths of hair from the weft that match that measurement. You'll layer these pieces to make one thick extension.

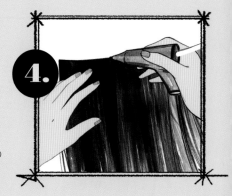

4. Layer the pieces on top of one another. Use the glue gun to glue the lengths together at the topstitching. Only glue two pieces together at a time. Add 1 or 2 inches (2.5 or 5 centimeters) of glue and press the pieces together. Go slowly so the hair aligns well.

5. Wait a few minutes for the glue to dry. Pull off any extra, stringy pieces of glue.

6. Add the wig clips. Place them comb-side up 1 or 2 inches apart along the top of the hair length. These clips snap open and shut to secure the hair to your head.

7. Using the needle and the thread, sew the clips onto the hairpiece. Bring the needle back and forth through the holes, pulling tightly. Then tie off the thread in a secure knot.

8. You're ready to add the extension to your hair. You want your natural hair to cover the extension's clips. So section off a layer of hair in a line across the top of your head. Pin or clip that hair out of your way.

9. Pop open the clips on the hair extension. Slide the combs into place on your head. Snap each clip shut. Pull on the extension gently to make sure it's secure.

10. Repeat with any other extensions you want to add.

11. Let your hair fall over the extensions. Finger-comb through your hair and the extensions to blend everything together. Check out your thicker, longer new 'do!

Chapter 3
HAIRSTYLING

Your haircut is only the beginning of your personal style. You can change your hairstyle every day. Or you can find a look that's a keeper, plus some variations for special occasions. From color to braids to updos, your hair can be all kinds of fabulous!

COLOR CRAZES

Looking to give your hair a color makeover? Got a thumbs-up from a parent or a guardian? Then you're probably ready to hit the salon for a dye job. But that's not your only option.

You might try a kit at home instead. You can make your hair lighter, darker, or a whole new shade. But it's a commitment. New color can last for weeks or months. It also damages your hair.

Color can be short-term too, though. Hair chalk and colored hair spray wash out with the next shampoo. Clip-in fashion hair adds instant streaks of color that are easily removed. Check around to compare these products' prices at stores and online. Start with an inexpensive option. If you like the results, save up to restock or upgrade your coloring supplies.

PAINT-ON COLOR

To give your hair a simple, easy-to-undo color change, paint on some color with eye shadow and leave-in conditioner. Add as many colors as you want—from neon green to shimmery blue. Remember, lighter colors show up better on dark hair.

What You Need:

- powdered eye shadow or pigment in fun colors
- leave-in hair conditioner
- a small mixing cup
- a spoon
- a small paintbrush
- a hairbrush
- hair spray

Here's How:

1. Mix equal parts of eye shadow or pigment and leave-in conditioner in the small cup. If the eye shadow is pressed, scrape the powder with the spoon.

2. Mix well until the powder is dissolved. The mixture should be liquid and not very thick.

3. Section off the part of your hair that you want to color. Paint on the color using the paintbrush.

4. Let the color dry on your hair for a few minutes.

5. Lightly brush or comb through your hair to remove clumps of color.

6. Spray some hair spray over the colored pieces. The color is set until your next shampoo.

EVERYDAY FLAIR HAIR

No matter what color your hair is, you can make it new and surprising each day. And with many styles, you don't have to worry about your hair falling flat, frizzing out, or even getting tousled by the wind. Just pull it back, pin it up, or twist it out of the way. It'll stay stylish while you focus on the rest of your life.

Braids. Whether they're carefree and messy or sleek and tight, braids can keep your hair under control and give you a unique look. Tiny braids and cornrows work for short hair. Fishtail braids, French braids, and waterfall braids are just a few of the styles you can try with long and medium locks.

Buns. Simple buns, high or low, are totally chic. A woven bun called a chignon rests at the nape of the neck. A French twist is when the hair is rolled into a long bun and pinned up in the back.

Dreadlocks. Dreads are matted, narrow sections of hair twisted together from roots to ends. The twists are held together with wax or oil. This makes ropelike strands around your head. It works well with thick, stiff hair. For finer, straighter hair, you could get a dread perm. This is a chemical process that changes your hair. If you don't want a full head of dreadlocks, you might just try one or two dread extensions. If you get dreads, you'll be living with them for a while. In most cases, the only way to remove them is to cut them out.

KNOTTED BRAID

This unusual braid uses knots instead of woven hair. It works well with long and medium lengths.

What You Need:

- hair-smoothing serum
- a clear hairband
- hair spray

Here's How:

1. Apply smoothing serum to your hair.

2. Part hair into two equal sections. Pull the two sections to one side of your head.

3. Neatly tie the two sections into a knot.

4. Knot the ends again. Keep adding more knots to suit your length.

5. Secure the ends with the hairband. Pull on different sections of the hair to loosen them.

6. Once you have a knotted look that you like, spritz with hair spray to set your look.

Braiding Tips

You want braids to be tight, but not *too* tight—or you could start losing your hair. Work slowly and carefully. Don't yank too hard. Use smoothing serum to keep hair soft.

PARTY HAIR!

A special occasion is the time for very special hairstyles. Whether you're heading to a formal event or having fun at a friend's place, the right 'do can really come in handy. You need a style that stays in place while you're accepting that award or jamming to that dance music. And you also want a look that sets you apart from the crowd. That's why updos are such classic party standbys.

An updo is any style that keeps your hair out of your face. Even simple buns, either high or low, look chic. Use a little hair spray to help your style set, so you can be sure it'll last as long as the party does!

BRAIDED FAUX HAWK

It's totally rocking, but it's oh-so faux. Just like a mohawk, a faux hawk gives you a fierce look. And it'll stay secure while you're out on the town! The best part? Unlike with a mohawk, you can switch to another style the next day.

What You Need:
- a rat-tail comb
- bobby pins
- a ponytail holder
- hair spray
- a mirror

Here's How:

1. Comb or brush through your hair. Get rid of any tangles.

2. Comb your hair back at the top and make a little bump in the front.

3. Pin your hair in place at the center of your head.

4. Right behind the bump, grab a section of hair. Separate it into three pieces.

5. Cross the right piece under the middle piece.

6. Cross the left piece under the middle piece.

7. Repeat the crossing pattern, working toward the back of your head. Pick up more hair from each side as you braid. You'll end up with an inside-out French braid.

8. Braid all the way down your head to the ends of your hair. Secure with a ponytail holder.

9. With the thin end of the comb, pull out pieces of hair from the braid.

10. Back-comb the loose pieces. Fluff them up and spray with hair spray. This makes the braid look like a mohawk. Check it out!

Short Hawk

If you have short hair, you can still make a faux hawk. Separate some hair from the rest along the top of your head. Use gel or pomade to slick the sides down and back. Use hair spray and a comb to tease the hair on top. Shape it like a mohawk and spray to make it hold.

Chapter 4
HAIR CANDY

Creative styling can do wonders for your hair. But you don't have to stop there. It's time to add some hair candy—a.k.a. accessories. From headbands to scarves to sparkly clips, accessories add color, bling, and a real *wow* factor to your hair. They're fun to wear and can reflect your mood or style for the day. Best of all, you can make them yourself!

DOUBLE-KNOTTED HEADBAND

A headband can be a real hair saver when you have no time for styling. Just slide one in and smooth your hair back. It's easy elegance in seconds! Turn an old T-shirt and fabric scraps into a supercute headband.

What You Need:

- an old T-shirt
- a measuring tape
- scissors
- small fabric remnants, ribbon, or embroidery thread

Here's How:

1. Lay the T-shirt out flat. Cut two horizontal 1-inch-wide (2.5 cm) strips from one side of the shirt to the other.

2. Stretch the T-shirt strips. They will get longer and thinner and curl at the edges.

3. Lay one strip on your work surface. Shape it into a loop. Overlap the ends. The ends should face toward you.

4. Lay the other strip in a U-shape on top of the loop. The ends should face away from you.

5. Pull out the bottom right end of the loop and lay it over the U-shaped strip.

6. Pull the upper left end of the U-shaped strip under the top of the loop-shaped strip.

7. Pick up the upper right end of the U-shaped strip. Pull it under the other end of the U-shaped strip where it sits in the middle of the loop-shaped strip.

8. Pull all ends of the strips outward to tighten the knot. Pull slowly and make sure the strips have equal lengths.

9. Cut a 1-inch-wide, 3- to 5-inch-long (7.6 to 13 cm) strip from the sleeve of the T-shirt. Tie it through the open loops of the headband.

10. Time to decorate your headband! Cut short, skinny strips from the rest of the fabric. You can also cut lengths of ribbon or embroidery thread.

11. Tie the smaller fabric pieces around your headband. Knot them on top and let the frayed ends fall down along the headband. Or knot them under and trim the ends for neat blocks of color. You can even do bows. Or find other ways to make your headband unique!

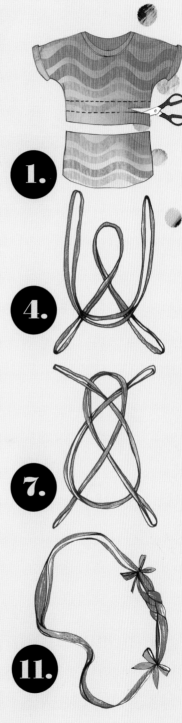

SCARVES AND HATS

Having a bad hair day? A hat or a scarf can be your stylish solution. Both cover up unruly hair and add a hip look. And what if your hair looks fine but could use some extra pizazz? In that case, a hat or a scarf can help show off and spruce up your lovely locks.

These accessories can fall anywhere on the spectrum from casual to fancy. Baseball caps are comfy and sturdy. Knit caps look great and help keep you warm in the winter. Fedoras and flat caps can be funky and fun.

Scarves offer plenty of variety too. You can fold a scarf into a thinner headband shape. Let its long ends dangle down into your hair. Or you can cover your hair completely. Experiment with different kinds of knots.

If you don't already have these accessories in your closet, no need to run to the mall. Look for bargain prices on vintage scarves and hats at thrift stores and garage sales. Or if you've got an old, worn-out shirt with an awesome pattern, try cutting it up to make a scarf from scratch.

TYING A SCARF

It's super easy to tie a scarf for a cute look. Here's how:

1. Use a square scarf. Fold it into a triangle.

2. Fold the triangle into a 2-inch-wide (5 cm) strip.

3. Wrap the strip around your head, near the nape of your neck. Position the middle of the strip at the back of your head. Bring the ends together in the front, near your forehead.

4. Tie the strip in a simple knot at the front. Try shifting the knot a little to one side.

5. Clip the scarf in place. Use a couple of bobby pins behind your ears. What an easy vintage look!

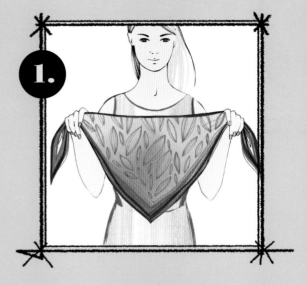

A LITTLE BLING

Want to add a touch of sparkle or a bit of glam to your hair? With clips and barrettes, you can put feathers, jewels, or flowers in your hair. Side combs can also add some color or sparkle.

It's a snap to create unique clips, barrettes, and combs. Just use a hot glue gun and attach your favorite materials to plain accessories. Add sequins or feathers. Use ribbon to cover the tops of clips and barrettes. Add crystals to side combs. Or see what you can do with embroidery floss. Check out local craft stores, bead stores, or thrift stores for supplies.

STRING COLOR-BLOCKED SIDE COMBS

Jazz up plain side combs with blocks of colored embroidery floss!

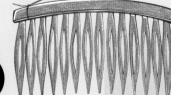

What You Need:

- two side combs
- embroidery floss in two or more colors
- scissors

Here's How:

1. Cut two 2-foot-long (0.6-meter) pieces of each colored thread. You will use one piece of each color for each comb.

2. Start with one comb. Tie a piece of embroidery floss at one end of the comb. Trim the short end.

3. Wrap the floss around the comb. Keep wrapping until you want to switch to a new color. Then knot the floss and trim the end.

4. Knot a new color of floss onto the comb. Trim the short end.

5. Add more colors in wide or narrow strips. Experiment to see what you like best.

6. Keep going until the comb's edge is completely covered with floss. Then make a matching comb to complete the pair.

6.

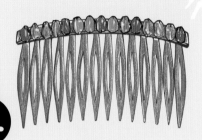

The Real Secret

Accessories are just one part of your complete hair look. With good hair health and care, a great cut, and some styling secrets, you can create the hair look that fits your personality.

Have fun trying out different looks. You never know—you may love a look you never even expected to like. Find inspiration online, in fashion magazines, or just by checking out your friends' looks. There's a whole world of styles out there waiting for you to discover them!

GLOSSARY

back-comb: to comb hair toward the scalp

cornrow: a flat braid worn close to the head

extension: a hairpiece that makes your hair look longer

flatter: to make you look good

frizz: hair that is in tight curls or has small tufts

hold: firmness or ability to stay in place

ions: atoms that have an electric charge

leave-in conditioner: a type of hair conditioner, often in a spray form, that doesn't need to be rinsed out

mohawk: a hairstyle in which the sides of the head are shaved, leaving a long strip of hair down the middle of the head from front to back

nutrients: substances that living things need to grow and stay healthy

synthetic: artificially made instead of naturally

texture: how smooth or rough something is

weft: a hair extension that can be glued, clipped, or taped to hair

FURTHER INFORMATION

"Hairstyle Ideas": *Seventeen*
http://www.seventeen.com/beauty/hair-ideas
Learn about the latest teen haircuts and styling tips on this site.

"Hair": *Teen Vogue*
http://www.teenvogue.com/beauty/hair?intcid=nav/beauty/hair
Find out about the latest styles for the next school dance or see celebrity photos for hair inspiration.

Kenney, Karen Latchana. *Skin Care & Makeup Tips & Tricks*. Minneapolis: Lerner Publications, 2016. Discover more ways to look your best with secrets for healthy skin and stylish makeup.

Krull, Kathleen. *Big Wig: A Little History of Hair*. New York: Arthur A. Levine Books, 2011. Learn about hairstyles from ancient Egypt up to modern times in this book.

Mayost, Eric. *Fabulous Teen Hairstyles: A Step-by-Step Guide to 34 Beautiful Styles*. New York: Sterling, 2013. Check out this book for more fun styles you can try with friends.

Rau, Dana Meachen. *Braiding Hair*. Ann Arbor, MI: Cherry Lake Publishing, 2013. Follow the activities in this book to dress up your hair with awesome braids.

INDEX

PHOTO ACKNOWLEDGMENTS

The images in this book are used with the permission of: © Subbotina Anna/Shutterstock.com, pp. 1 (right), 4 (bottom), (top), 31; © KK-Foto/Shutterstock.com, p. 1 (left); © Sukharevskyy Dmytro (nevodka)/Shutterstock.com, pp. 3, 8; © mates/Shutterstock.com, p. 6 (top) © John McQueen/Shutterstock.com, p. 6 (bottom right); © Pavel V Mukhin/Shutterstock.com, p. 6 (bottom left); © Africa Studio/Shutterstock.com, pp. 10, 30; © natsa/Shutterstock.com, p. 14; © Login/Shutterstock.com, p. 16; © Color Symphony/Shutterstock.com, p. 18; © plearn/Shutterstock.com, p. 20; © LiliGraphie/Shutterstock.com, p. 22; © Loskutnikov/Shutterstock.com, p. 24; © Kaya/Shutterstock.com, p. 26 (top); © TerraceStudio/Shutterstock.com, p. 26 (bottom); © severija/Shutterstock.com, p. 28; © Ragnarock/Shutterstock.com, p. 29 (middle), (bottom); © LiliGraphie/Shutterstock.com, p. 32.

Front cover: © Africa Studio/Shutterstock.com, (hair brushes); © Subbotina Anna/Shutterstock.com (red hair curls); © Dimedrol68/Shutterstock.com (hair dryer); © Subbotina Anna/Shutterstock.com (black hair curl).

Back cover: © severija/Shutterstock.com (gold glitter); © KK-Foto/Shutterstock.com (black hair curl); © mates/Shutterstock.com (bobby pins); © Pavel V Mukhin/Shutterstock.com (hairbands).